CRABTREE
CONTACT

HI TECH WORLD:
COOL
STUFF

Ben Hubbard

werboard

Crabtree Publishing Company
www.crabtreebooks.com

Crabtree Publishing Company

www.crabtreebooks.com

1-800-387-7650

PMB 59051
350 Fifth Avenue, 59th Floor
New York, NY, 10118

616 Welland Avenue,
St. Catharines, Ontario
L2M 5V6

Content development by
Shakespeare Squared

www.ShakespeareSquared.com

Published by
Crabtree Publishing
Company © 2010

First published
in Great Britain in
2010 by TickTock
Entertainment Ltd.

Printed in the
U.S.A./122009
CG20091120

Crabtree Publishing
Company credits:
Project manager: Kathy Middleton
Editor: Reagan Miller
Production coordinator: Katherine Berti
Prepress technician: Katherine Berti

TickTock credits:
Publisher: Melissa Fairley
Art director: Faith Booker
Editor: Victoria Garrard
Designer: Emma Randall
Production controller: Ed Green
Production manager: Suzy Kelly

Thank you to Lorraine Petersen and the members of nasen

Picture credits (t=top; b=bottom; c=centre; l=left; r=right; OFC=outside front cover;
OBC=outside): Sharon Bobrow: 19 (main). Courtesy of AbsolutelyNew, Inc.: 13t. Courtesy
of Artanova: 13b. Courtesy of Gerald W. Winkler (http://www.gekkomat.de): 18. Courtesy
of Hybra Advance Technology and AbsolutelyNew, Inc.: 26 (both). Courtesy of iHouse
Tecnologia Ltda (www.ihouse.com.br): 12. Courtesy of LG: 27 (both). Courtesy of Rubato
Productions via Concerthands.com: 23. Courtesy of Scarpar Pty Ltd.: 1, 14–15 (all). Courtesy
of YikeBike: 16 (all). Fabien Cousteau: 29 (both). Michael Crabtree/Reuters/Corbis: 24–25.
Firebox.com: 2, 11 (both), 21. Luis Galvez: 19bl. Mike Hoover: 5b, 28. Nick Shotter (inventor
and builder of 4MO): 17. © Nadine Meisel & Ena Macana 2005: 10. Copyright (©), 2009
Hybrid Recognition Technologies, Ltd, All rights reserved: 4, 9. Shutterstock: OFC, 6 (dog),
22, OBC. Sam Toren/Alamy: 8. Uncle Milton Industries: 7 (all). Used by permission of
Sony Electronics Inc.: 5t, 20. www.RoamEOforPets.com: 6 (dog collar and GPS).

Every effort has been made to trace copyright holders, and we apologize in advance
for any omissions. We would be pleased to insert the appropriate acknowledgments
in any subsequent edition of this publication.

Library and Archives Canada Cataloguing in Publication

Hubbard, Ben
     Hi tech world : cool stuff / Ben Hubbard.

(Crabtree contact)
Includes index.
ISBN 978-0-7787-7529-4 (bound).--ISBN 978-0-7787-7551-5 (pbk.)

     1. Inventions--Juvenile literature. I. Title. II. Series:
Crabtree contact

T48.H82 2010   j600   C2009-907050-2

Library of Congress Cataloging-in-Publication Data

Hubbard, Ben.
  Hi tech world. Cool stuff / Ben Hubbard.
       p. cm. -- (Crabtree contact)
  Includes index.
  ISBN 978-0-7787-7551-5 (pbk. : alk. paper)
  -- ISBN 978-0-7787-7529-4 (reinforced library binding : alk. paper)
  1. Inventions--Juvenile literature. I. Title. II. Title: Cool stuff. III.
Series.

T48.H77 2010
600--dc22

                                                            2009049078

The Clocky alarm

CONTENTS

INTRODUCTION

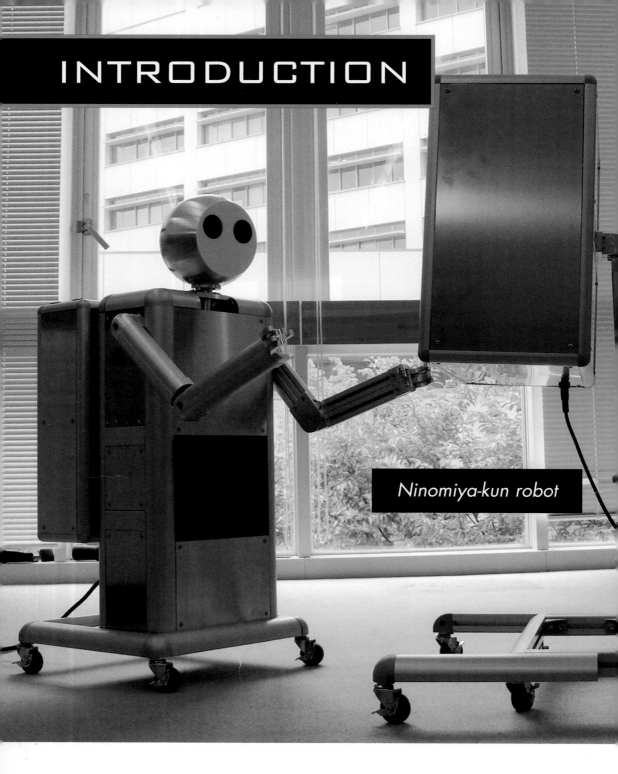

Ninomiya-kun robot

If you have ever hoped, dreamed, and wished for a cool new gadget to rock your world—look no further.

Sony® Party-shot™

Used by permission of Sony Electronics Inc.

Troy shark submarine

Talking robots, spinning cameras, and shark submarines are no longer just daydreams. Read on for a sensational roundup of the latest gizmos and gadgets.

PETS

Ever had a pet dog that ran away—despite your calls, shouts, and screams?

Now you can find your lost pet with the RoamEO™ dog collar. A hand-held screen tracks the dog up to 3.1 miles (five kilometers) away, using a **GPS (Global Positioning System)**.

RoamEO™ dog collar

GPS

Have you ever wondered what your pet does when you are not around? The Pet's Eye View™ camera attaches to your pet's collar and can be set to take a picture every one, ten, or 15 minutes.

Pet's Eye View™

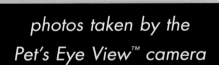

photos taken by the Pet's Eye View™ camera

ROBOTS

This new robot looks and moves just like a real fish.

However, this fish has a purpose—it finds **pollution** in **harbors**. The 4.9-foot (1.5-meter) long robot can detect pollution, such as an oil spill. It then **transmits** a warning back to scientists on shore.

If you have ever wanted to keep reading but your eyelids are drooping, this robot can take over for you. The 3.2-foot (one-meter) high Japanese Ninomiya-kun robot reads books using its camera eyes. It uses text-recognition software to read the words and speaks through a voice **synthesizer**.

Ninomiya-kun robot

ALARM CLOCKS

Do you have trouble getting up in the morning? These alarm clocks may be just what you need!

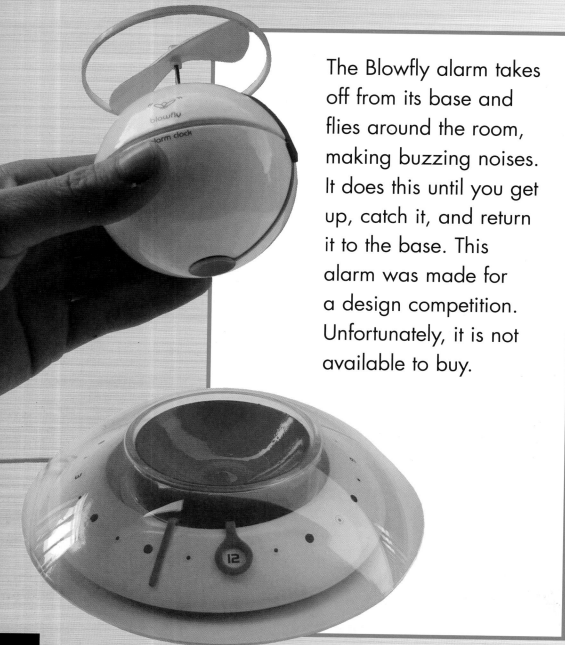

The Blowfly alarm takes off from its base and flies around the room, making buzzing noises. It does this until you get up, catch it, and return it to the base. This alarm was made for a design competition. Unfortunately, it is not available to buy.

The Clocky® alarm rolls off your bedside table and travels around your room, all while its alarm beeps loudly. The only option is to get out of bed, find it, and turn it off.

AT HOME

If you like your water temperature and pressure to be perfect, but cannot be bothered to keep adjusting the taps— this is for you!

The Smartfaucet™ recognizes your face and adjusts the water temperature and pressure to your personal settings. The screen also displays your email and a calendar, all while you are washing up.

Have you ever woken up in the night and had to stumble around looking for the doorknob? The Illumi-knob™ might be the gadget for you! It attaches to your door handle and turns on a dim light if it senses movement.

The Athena sofa contains a computer, a wireless connection, an ipod™ **dock**, an MP3 player, and built-in loudspeakers. Inside each armrest is a flat-screen monitor and keyboard, ready to pop out at your command.

SKATEBOARD

The Scarpar Powerboard™ is a motorized **board that uses** tracked wheels **to cruise** over almost any surface—from rocky ground to sand or snow.

The Scarpar Powerboard™ will be able to reach a top speed of 37 miles per hour (60 kilometers per hour)!

The YikeBike™ is a folding electric bicycle. It will run for about half an hour on a 30 minute battery charge.

- 20-inch (51-centimeter) front wheel
- motor: 1.5 kw electric
- weight: 22 pounds (10 kilograms)
- nano-**lithium**-phosphate battery
- 30 minute charge time
- range: 5.5-6.2 miles (9–10 kilometers)
- electronic anti-skid brakes
- hand grips featuring indicators, lights and controls
- top speed: 12.4 miles per hour (20 kilometers per hour)

The YikeBike™ folds up neatly.

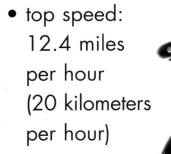

**The 4MC is a four-wheeled motorbike.
It is much safer than two-wheeled bikes.**

- four wheels
- motor: 125**cc**–400cc
- weight: 353–440 pounds (160–200 kilograms)
- width: 22.8 inches (58 centimeters)—
  the same as a two-wheeled bike
- features an anti-tilting device which
  means the bike can lean over at an
  incredible angle without tipping over

GETTING UP AND DOWN

The Gekkomat turns you into a genuine wall climber, like a lizard—or Spider-Man®.

The vacuum pads attach to your feet and hands and use suction to secure you tightly onto a wall. The suction is created using air from a tank on your back.

Rescue Reel can help you escape from the top of a high-rise building. Like a giant fishing reel, a strong cord unravels slowly, letting you climb down the side of the building.

CAMERAS

The Sony® Party-shot™ device rotates, tilts, and zooms the Cyber-shot™ camera. This camera then uses facial-recognition technology to know when to take pictures. This technology allows the camera to scan and then focus on facial features before taking the picture.

Cyber-shot™ camera

Sony® Party-shot™ device

The Veho™ Muvi™ Micro DV Camcorder is so small, it has room for only one button—record. The 2.2-inch (5.5-centimeter) long video recorder can hang from your neck or even attach to a helmet to record while you play sports.

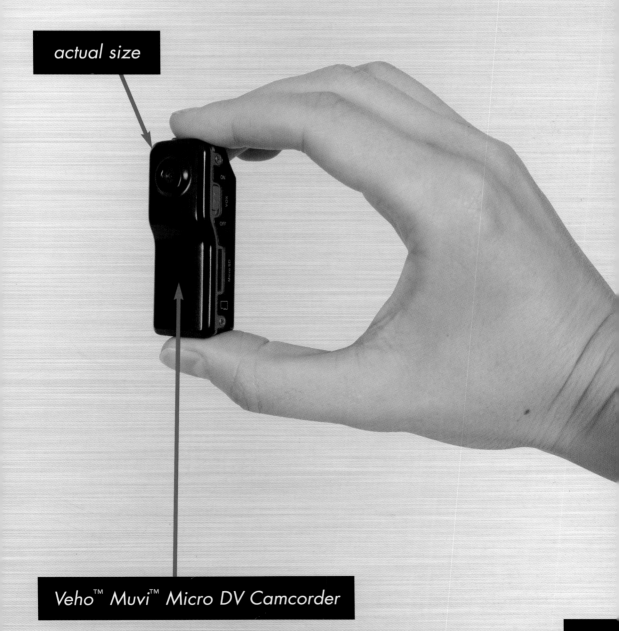

actual size

Veho™ Muvi™ Micro DV Camcorder

ENTERTAINMENT

Would you like to jump 6.5 feet (two meters) into the air or run at more than 24.8 miles per hour (40 kilometers per hour)?

Powerbocks are spring-loaded **stilts** that attach to your feet. Experts say that with only 30 minutes of practice, you too can become a human kangaroo!

Practice may be the most boring part of learning to play the piano. But help is now here! The Concert Hands™ system guides your hands along a track in front of the keyboard. A gentle **pulse** in the finger gloves lets you know when to hit each key.

Concert Hands™ teaching system

THE AQUADA

The Gibbs Aquada is a high-speed vehicle that can travel both in water and on land. Just drive it into the water and you are sailing away!

- transforms from car to boat in six seconds
- top speed of 100 miles per hour (160 kilometers per hour) on land
- top speed of 31 miles per hour (50 kilometers per hour) in water
- jet-propulsion system
- **V6** four-speed engine

People normally connect their bluetooth devices to their cell phones and wear them on their ears.

The ORB™ **bluetooth** headset can also be worn as a ring.

The ORB™ ring also displays things like caller ID and calendar information.

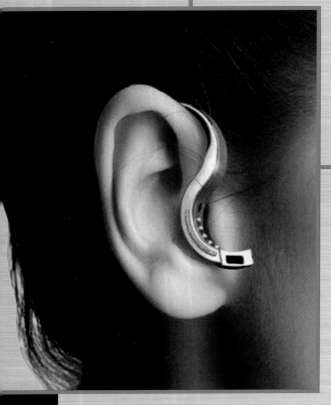

For those who want to make a call from their watch, the LG-GD910™ is for you. This touch-screen watch/phone has everything you could wish for, including a camera and an MP3 player.

SHARK SUBMARINE

"Troy" is a submarine built to look, move, and even behave like a great white shark. It was designed to get as close as possible to the massive predator in its natural environment.

"The whole point is to fool them into thinking I'm a shark."
– Fabien Cousteau, inventor

Troy specs:
- weight: 1,201 pounds (545 kilograms)
- length: 14.1 feet (4.3 meters)
- plastic, rubber, and elastic skin
- three cameras
- escape hatch in the head for a quick exit
- silent movement
- The passenger requires a **wet suit** and scuba-diving gear to breathe.

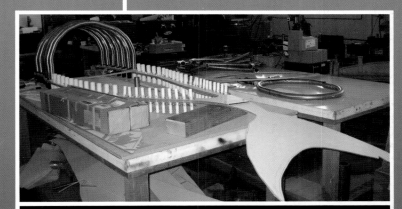

Troy's ribs are made of stainless-steel. Each rib is 1.9 inches (five centimeters) wide.

NEED-TO-KNOW WORDS

bluetooth Wireless technology used for transferring information at high speeds

cc Cubic centimeters; used to measure the size of an engine

dock A platform or base for an electronic device

GPS (Global Positioning System) A navigation system based on information sent from satellites around the planet

harbor A sheltered area of water where ships or other watercraft can dock

lithium (battery) Describes a rechargeable battery that uses the metallic element lithium; provides twice the energy of an ordinary battery

motorized Something that has a motor added to make it go faster

pollution Contamination of the environment due to human activities

pulse A gentle vibration at regular intervals

stilts Upright poles that attach to the feet to allow the user to walk high above the ground

synthesizer A machine that electronically produces sounds

tracked wheels Wheels with a system of continuous tracks surrounding it for a better grip on rough areas

transmit To broadcast or send out information

V6 A six-cylinder engine

wet suit A tight-fitting rubber suit that helps to keep the wearer warm in cold water

DID YOU KNOW?

- In 1943, the president of IBM, Thomas Watson, said he thought there was a market for only five computers worldwide.

- In 1946, movie executive Darryl Zanuck predicted television would be dead within six months of it being released.

- In 2004, Microsoft founder Bill Gates said there would be no more spam emails by 2006.

- In 1876, the head of the British Post Office said the United States may need telephones but Great Britain did not—it had plenty of messenger boys instead.

COOL STUFF ONLINE

Here are some Web sites dedicated to the latest technology in gadgets and electronics:

http://gizmodo.com

www.coolest-gadgets.com

www.engadget.com

www.gadgetmadness.com

www.gizmoactive.com

www.wired.com

Publisher's note to educators and parents:
Our editors have carefully reviewed these Web sites to ensure that they are suitable for children. Many Web sites change frequently, however, and we cannot guarantee that a site's future contents will continue to meet our high standards of quality and educational value. Be advised that children should be closely supervised whenever they access the Internet.

INDEX